Becoming

Becoming

⁂

Mother Poems
By
Maria Brady-Smith

Zoe Press
Washington, Missouri
2011

Zoe Press
Washington, Missouri
63090

© 2011 by Maria Brady-Smith
All rights reserved
Printed in the United States of America

Contact Information:
mariabradysmith@gmail.com

ISBN 978-0-615-41401-0

*For Clara, Laurel and Grace-
and all the ways that we have
formed each other*

Introduction

This book is a compilation of poems that I have written throughout twenty-five years of mothering. As is true for most of us, I came into the job completely naive, believing that I could just move over a bit to make room for children and that my life would otherwise go on as usual. I had no idea how completely their presence would transform me.

One of the interesting things about being a mother is that the job is constantly changing because children are constantly changing. In the beginning, it was about adapting to their very presence, to the incredible love and to the overwhelming responsibility that I felt. In the middle, I was so absorbed in the details of the daily-ness that I could barely find time for anything else. As my children grow up and move away, I am learning, once again, that there is much more to me than being a mom. Thus, there is a theme of change and letting go throughout these pages.

These poems are, necessarily, personal. I can only write from my own experience as a mother. I am aware that there are as many ways to parent as there are parents. But in my countless conversations with other parents, no matter how similar or different our circumstances, I always feel a common, inexplicable bond. I hope the reader can feel that, too.

This compilation is, of course, not complete. For every moment that I put on paper, there are thousands that I did not capture, too busy living it to grab a pen before it floated away and the next one came along.

I would like to thank my daughter, Laurel, for the cover painting and Megan Ruff and my son-in-law, Matt Wilson for the cover design. Thanks to all my family and friends who contributed photographs, all beautiful pictures of parenthood.

Thank you to Katie Borders, Jane Humphreys, Liz Williams and my daughter, Clara Wilson for your excellent editing assistance. Thank you to my daughter, Grace Smith, for your technical assistance and sound advise. Thank you to Gloria Bauermeister, Robin Morgan and Chris Stuckenschneider for your endless support and encouragement. Lastly, I would like to thank my husband Mike, for believing that I am better than I really am. Your belief gives me courage.

Table of Contents

Becoming	15
Baby at Midnight	16
playing house	17
Bedtime for a Two-Year Old	18
I'm the Mom	20
Makeover by My Daughter age 4	22
Night Call	23
Pretend Play	24
Laurel went to kindergarten today	26
In the Details	28
A Vision	33
Wonder Lost	34
Morning	37
End of the Day	38
Camera	39
The Dance	41
Missing My Daughters	43
After the Car Wreck	44
House	46
Popular	47
Ingredients	49

Singing in the Shower	50
Wrecking Ball	51
At Thirteen	52
Time	53
Unsaid	55
Induction	56
I Reach Up	57
Other Life	58
Nourish	61
Photographs	62
Your Hands	64
I Hurt My Back	65
Daughter-Leaving	66
You Again	68
Dog	70
Twenty-Seven Years Later	71
Sweet Pea	72
25	73
Now	74
Surprise	76
Hello, Poppy Seed	78

Becoming

Becoming

In your womb
she rests,
drawing from blood, bone
all she needs.
Your heart calls hers
to sing its rhythm.

Your fear,
the losses you've sustained
cannot touch her here.
She grows safely,
formed in perfect
warmth,
silence,
darkness.

She forms you, too,
calling forth a self
you didn't know you possessed.
Your mind and heart
grow strong
around her.

Baby at Midnight

My need is for that crying baby
To hold against the coldness
Of my breast.
My newly born one
Whose face and hands
And quivering lips
Move me
To the quietest place of my soul.
We go there together,
Just she and I.
The world around
Becomes a dark shadow
That cannot touch us.
Her mouth searches and I give.
Her tiny hand
Curls around my finger
As I stroke.
She, unaware
Of how I drink her in.
This is all I know for now.
This is all she's known
Forever.
A moment of union
In a world of separation.

playing house

ok you be the baby and I'll be the mommy let's say you wake up crying and I come to your crib in the night oh you're so hot baby you must be sick don't worry mommy will take care of you let's pretend that I bring you to the doctor so he can make you well he looks in your ears and he listens to your heart and he gives you some medicine I take you home and hold you and rock you and let's say you just cry and cry because you feel so bad oh my poor little baby mommy is here I love you I love you I love you so much I sing you a little song and finally you fall asleep you've been sick for a very long time now let's pretend you get better ok I said let's pretend you get better hey its my turn remember that is the way we play this game no fair I'm really tired and I need a nap and I don't feel well at all and I just want to cry and how come there's nobody to take care of me

Bedtime for a Two Year Old

I sit in the rocker and pick her up.
She snuggles down into her spot,
A perfect fit in the curve of my arm.
I draw my knees up around her,
Cover us both with her blanky.
We rock for a few minutes
Looking at each other
And then she says,
"Sing."

"What do you want me to sing?" I ask.
She thinks for a moment and replies,
"Animals," or "Angels,"
And I know which one she means.
I sing and she sings along
Even though she doesn't know the words.
" 'nother song,"
She says when I finish.

"OK, one more
And then it's time to go night-night."
"One more," she agrees.
But when that song is over,
She says it again,
Hopeful.
Sometimes I give in and sing another.
Sometimes not.

There is a part of me
That would also like to stay here all night
Rocking
My growing-up-too-fast baby
Drifting into the world of sleep.

I'm the Mom

I wasn't born a mother,
Like my children think.

Once,
Not long ago,
I was a child, too.
I hung my head off the couch
And looked at the world
Upside down,
Lost myself in play,
Picked at meals set in front of me,
Whined because my favorite dress
Was still in the laundry.

Now, small eyes look to me
For protection,
Comfort, sustenance
Assuming I can provide it all.

I worry I'm doing it wrong,
That they're not having
A good childhood,
Or that I'll lose myself completely
In this process.

But the bottom line is—
They need me to be the mom.
There are no other options.

So everyday, I get up
And do the best I can.
Sometimes it flows from me
Like honey,
Sometimes it feels
Like a thousand bees
Swarming.

That's all.
No natural ability, no formula.
I just look at those beautiful faces
Trusting
That I was born this way
And I know
I have to become
What they believe
I am.

Makeover by My Daughter, age 4

She leans against me,
Her belly, warm bread dough against my knees,
Breathing hard with concentration,
The serious eyes of an artist
Close enough to paint my every pore.

Her delicate fingers swipe
Powdered brush across my skin.
Beside her
Lies the magical compact
With its turquoise, pinks
And sparkly silvers,
Which she applies
Indiscriminately,
Tickling my cheeks and lips
And eyelids,
Dipping again and again
For a thick film of color.

"There."

She stands back
To view her masterpiece,
Proudly brings the mirror
To show me
The crazy aging clown
She has created.

Night Call

Something calls for me
Late at night,
Wakes me to feel
The world—
Silent,
This home—
Peaceful, undemanding,
My children—
Safe,
Insulated by darkness.
I walk softly through this hour,
My vigilance left resting,
And hear the delicate whisper
Of being.

Pretend Play

She sits across the room,
Her back to me,
A doll in each hand,
Mommy doll and child doll
Voices soft and solicitous
Or cruel and demanding.

This room, these giant sticks
Of furniture, even I
Do not exist.

I cradle that world in memory
But I can no longer enter there.
If I move toward her,
I will crash through
Those boundaries of pretend,
And she will look down,
Self-consciously,
And stop her play.

So I listen from a distance
Pretending
To be engrossed in my book.

She discovers all her selves there—
The poor sweet orphan child,
The mean-spirited sister
And all the others in between.
She plays out stories
That have painted themselves
On her mind

And she tunes out perfectly
Thoughts unnecessary
To this moment.

Laurel went to kindergarten today

She just hopped on the bus
And went away.

I wanted to tell her a lot of things before she left
About how proud I am of her,
And how I want her to do her best,
But she doesn't have to be perfect,
About how lucky we are
That she can go to school and learn
And that she is great
Just the way she is.

But I knew I'd cry
So I just gave her a big hug
And told her I loved her.
I watched her smile nervously
Before she disappeared into the mouth
Of that big bus.

Then I came home to this empty house.
It is quiet and dark and gloomy
And I need a child
To share my day.

We would turn on the lamp
And sit on the couch.
She'd snuggle close,
We'd open a book
And feel good to be alone together.

Instead,
I write this poem,
Try to remember silence
And wait for the bus
To bring her home again.

In the Details

It's in the details that I exist.
It's in good morning, did you sleep ok?
Come on girls, its time to wake up,
Flipping on the hall light
Shuffling down the stairs
To start coffee.
It's in that first morning book,
Reading light
On my end of the couch.
God, make this a good day.
It's in sleepy morning grumpy faces,
I don't want to go to school,
Warm cheek kiss
And messy hair, sour breath.
It's in I can't find my khakis,
We need lunch money,
Shower and dressing, now it's time to rush,
Come on, we'll be late
And mommy, hold you, hold you
Arms outstretched
Of the little one who can't understand hurry.
It's have a good day, I love you,
See you after school,
Then sweet babysitter home
Warm morning smells
And good-bye to the little one
Clinging tight.
It's in changing gears now
To my other world
Of folders and families
And phone calls
And lots and lots of people
With stories like mine,
Yet different.

It's driving,
Always driving
To get it all done
To get to the end of the list for today
Only to realize how much I forgot.
It's picking up kids
And picking up the house,
Wiping away tears
And wiping dried cereal off the table.
What's for dinner,
Throw in a load,
I've got homework,
Can you help?
I want a drink,
I'm starving,
We'll eat soon, no more cookies,
Will you read me a story?
And sometimes,
An unsolicited hug from a child.
I love you,
How was your day?
You're growing up too fast,
You can't be my baby,
You're as tall as I am.
Pass the potatoes,
Who has the dishes?
Switch a load,
When will I fold it?
A phone call, my friend's voice
That feels like the sunrise
Are you busy?
Let's get together soon.
It's bath time and
Did you brush your teeth?
These floors sure need sweeping.
Did you finish your homework?

Did you finish your room?
Asking these questions
But wondering inside
Are you happy?
Are you healthy?
Am I doing enough?
Can we read, Mom?
That sounds great
As soon as I'm finished…
It's sweet dreams,
I love you.
Is this the way it's supposed to be?
It's reading time writing time
Quiet on the couch.
God, thank you and help me,
Till my eyes won't stay open.
I crawl into bed,
My husband's warm breathing,
I love you, I miss you, I need you,
Good-night.

At the Airport

We say good-bye to you,
Kissing, hugging.
Grace bursts into tears, not knowing
That a flight across the country
Is no more than a drive across town.

"I'll be back soon," you say,
Reluctant to go.
"Have a great time, we'll miss you,"
Rushing you to leave—
And you do.

But then your face appears again
From the tunnel, searching.
And I wish I hadn't said
Those things days ago,
About the distance between us,
About how things weren't right,
How I'd given up on change.

Because in that brief moment,
I pictured us there as you would see us,
Your wife and daughters
Gathering ourselves, turning to leave.
Your eyes in that moment
Seemed to be pleading
Please don't go away,
Say that you'll love me forever.

Grace cries in my arms
Reaching for you and kicking.
I stand still trying to steady her,
And smile my strongest
We will be waiting.

A Vision

I see myself an old woman,
Lying, one morning,
On my deathbed.

It would be so clear then.

The painful things—
Wasted wanting, worries,
Time spent following some anxious call,
Dark roads of fear.

The things that were good
Would flash before me
Like stars—
Every moment with a child,
Walks with my husband,
Each hand held out to a friend,
Like a light in the universe.

And the tasks— menial, redundant
Wouldn't seem so bad after all,
But like pebbles on the path,
Order out of chaos.

Is this clarity only available
For those brief moments
At the end
Or can this vision
Shake clean my perspective
Like the fresh sheet of a day
Before me?

Wonder Lost

A child,
Born herself,
An observer,
Watches her world
With unique eyes,
Wondering, wondering.
As she grows,
She discovers within herself
A singular way of interacting.

She feeds a grasshopper grass,
She makes the dead moth a coffin
From kleenex and flower petals.
She draws and draws
The beautiful pictures
That come into her head.
She knows a God
That I never taught her
Because I do not see so clearly.
She waits patiently
For Him to hand her the hopes
That give her courage.
Scared of monsters,
She magically shrinks them
To fit in her hand.
She throws the bad ones away,
Keeping the nice ones for friends.
I try to give her direction
But often I am awed
By what she already knows.

She grows a little older
And it is time to go to school
Where expectations change.

There is no time for her to think
Of what the colorful construction paper
Wants to become
Because an adult stands in front of her
Directing her to put the red on white
To make an American Flag.
She stares at the numbers through tears,
Wondering how to make sense of them.
It is as if she has landed,
Ker-plunk,

On some distant planet
Where she can no longer
Find her smooth path.
She is exposed to evaluation,
A mirror set in front of her
Revealing only her faults,
And shame at the realization
That she is different
From these other ones.

She recoils like a snail
Inside her shell,
But we demand that she come out.
She fights this new world
By kicking and screaming at me.
Seeing that I don't change it,
She mourns
That gentle world where she could unfold.

Over the years she slowly relents,
Realizing that
This is a monster she cannot shrink.
She learns to perform,
Making approval her goal.

Her heart is not in it, though.
It is as if, every day,
She is trying to interpret a language
That she does not care about or understand.

I find her sometimes in her room
Staring out the window.
"What are you doing?" I ask.
"Nothing," she replies, blankly.
I think maybe she is looking
For someone she left behind
Yet can't quite remember.

Morning

Every morning, I wake you
With the same quiet call.
"Good morning, little pumpkin."
"Good morning, little monkey."

Rubbing your resistant back
And legs so warm from sleep.
I breathe you in,
Kiss your limp hand,
So happy, so happy
That you are here.

So blessed to be the one
Who calls you
Back into the world
Each morning.

End of the Day

And I am spent.
So many emotions
Have washed through
My body today
And left their residue behind.

A confusing soup of
Nervousness and laughter,
Contentedness and disappointment,
Relief and heartbreak
Has settled in my stomach.

Only sleep will
Sweep it all away.
Only my dreams will dissolve it.

Camera

This moment…
Startling and unpredictable and perfect.
As my heart fills with it,
My first thought
Is to run
And grab the camera,
To preserve every bit of it—
The glowing face of my child,
The way we are all together here,
The laughter and spontaneity.

And yet,
The camera isn't loaded,
Or simply running for that
Might destroy the wholeness
Of this.

And so,
I try to paint it on my mind,
To soak in every color,
Every sound.

But you know the faults of memory,
How the picture fades,
How it is lost in the jumble
Of constant activity.

I want so desperately
To hold onto this moment,
That even in its perfection
Something is taken.

Even as I live it,
I grieve its loss,
Knowing
That in a million years,
I could never
Purposefully recreate
A moment such as this.

The Dance

They walk onto the dance floor together—
A mother and her nine-year old daughter.
The mother smiles and swings,
Reaching automatically
For her daughter's hand.
They have danced like this
A hundred times before.

This time, however,
The daughter pulls back.
Hunching her shoulders
And crossing her arms,
She looks at her mother
As if she has never seen
Such foolishness.

The mother, confused,
Pursues.
She twirls and swoops,
Begging again
With her reaching hand.

The daughter glares now,
Her eyes screaming
For her mother to stop.

The mother does not understand
This new dance step.
What has happened to her child?

As she watches her mother dance alone,
The half grown girl's
Childish foot
Taps the rhythm
That still lives deep inside her.

Missing My Daughters

It is five am where they are,
So far away.
I can almost hear their vulnerable breathing,
Almost smell the sleepy rooms
Where they must still be dreaming.

I miss their presence around me.

I walk into their bedrooms and wonder
If they were ever really here at all
And what would I do
If they weren't— suddenly,
And what I will do
When they aren't— eventually.

I miss their presence around me.

They light up this home
With their spirits.
Every corner feels alive
When they are here.
Now, although it is quiet,
Their absence resounds.

I miss their presence around me.

After the Car Wreck

Weeks have passed now.
We're all settling down.
The impact is fading
Into achy muscles
And insurance claims.

Yet that moment replays itself.
The screaming wheels behind us,
The violent jolt jerking us
Into oncoming traffic,
Swerving back again,
The feeling of everything lost
In a stranger's brief thoughtlessness.

Then we are standing
Outside the crushed car,
Stunned,
While the world moves fast
Around us.
Cars whizzing by,
Sirens, ambulance, tow truck,
People are talking to me,
But I can't hear them.

My single focus
Is my children.
I grab onto them,
I survey their bodies.
Fear in their eyes,
Glass in their hair,

But not a single drop of blood,
Not a single broken bone.
How can that be?
I saw them in that car,
Surrounded by breaking glass,
Crushed metal…

It is only now that I can see Her
Hand on our tiny lives,
Gently caring,
Protecting Her children.

It is only now that I can hear Her
Quiet whisper
Below the screeching and chaos.

It is only now that I begin to understand.

I have the luxury
Of letting this event
Fade into the meandering
Story of our lives.

Awed, comforted by a Presence
Greater, more powerful,
Yet quieter
Than the crashing unknown.

House

 I like this house
When it is quiet,
When I have time
To sit and think.

I think of this house
As a place that has breathed us
In and out all these years,
A silent witness to our days.

Tender sweetness,
Conflict and tears,
This house has absorbed it all
With fortifying patience.

It has stored in its walls
As I have stored in my heart
Each new moment
Of each unfolding day.

Popular

At eleven,
My daughter has left behind
The world of pretend.
Now she stands on the brink
Of a new world—
The world of popular.

She sees kids she's known for years,
Defined in a whole new way—
By the clothes they wear
And the people they know.

I know the inevitable dangers
Of this world,
But I am powerless
To keep her sheltered from them.

I hold my breath
And hope for the best,
Unsure how to arm her
For the betrayals
She will encounter here.

I want to tell her—
If you make it in this world,
Don't lose your kindness.
If you don't,
Hold tight to your heart.

I want to tell her—
In a dozen years,
None of this will matter.
But I'm not so sure that is true.

Like most of us,
She will remember
The world of popular
And her place in it
For years to come.

Ingredients

Dusty day,
Waning sun,
Train in the distance,
Couch and table,
Sleeping dog curled beside me,
Glass of wine,
Half full.

Children gone for the evening,
Husband busy in the garden,
Pen and notebook,
Mind calm and stirring,
Silence.

Singing in the Shower

On her hidden stage
Behind that curtain,
Flowered with water,
She belts out
High notes,
Loud notes.

Her daring melodies
Float through the house,
A serenade
To the evening's activities.

After a very long performance,
The water stops
And from a cloud of fog,
She emerges,
Head wrapped in a towel,
Like the star that she is,
Cleansed inside and out
By singing
At the top of her lungs
In the shower.

Wrecking Ball

I hear about cancer
And I can almost feel the lump.
I see another family
Broken to pieces
And my home feels suddenly

Very fragile.

The wrecking ball swings past us
One more time
Hitting a neighbor,
A relative, a friend.

I stand still,
Silently checking myself, my family
Wondering if we are protected
By some invisible,
Indestructible shell

Or if that ball waits for us
Around some later corner,
Its momentum

Building with time.

At Thirteen

Who is this before me?
Today you come in,
Snapping your fingers,
Dancing,
Laughing into the phone.

Yesterday you were all tears
And insecurities,
Melting into your pillow.

And whose body is this?
Those hips with their perfect curve,
Smooth shoulder,
The flat belly
Inconspicuously revealed.

Yesterday you were
A long-legged gazelle,
Awkward and embarrassed
By your own presence.

Everyday you are someone new,
Wholly amazing and unexpected.
Every day I relearn your presence.

Time

That's all I want.
I don't need a fancy vacation
Or dinner at an expensive restaurant.
I just want the pressure
Of too much responsibility
Removed for one day.

I'd wake up that morning
Free from the list of details
Typing itself on my brain
And walk down the stairs
To rooms cleared of clutter.
Just a lamp, a plant,
A favorite book here or there.

Maybe what I want
Is for time to go away
And stop ordering me.
Instead I'll turn toward
That white pine in the yard
That has been tapping me
On the shoulder.
"Yes?" I'll say
And it will draw me
High into its branches.

Then I'll look down
And see my life
From a different place,
Just as it is.
I'll look at every little thing
Without thinking I need
To do something about it.

Maybe what I really want
Is to be two people,
One who can live it,
Take care of things
And one who can sit back
And just be.

Unsaid

My barely
Teenage daughter weeps.
Deep knotted sobs.
I ask her what is wrong
And she just replies,
"I don't know."
All my soothings
And proddings
Result in no enlightenment
For either of us,
Just a wrenching
"I don't know."

It's as if I have to reach her
On a different plane.
These words
Aren't working out.

I breathe,
Swim back into
Our deepest connection,
And we are silent together.
I let my hand on her knee listen,
Take in her world.

I try to give her
The only gift I can.
"I'm OK," I let my stillness tell her.
And hope she understands,
By heart,
That she will be OK,
Too.

Induction

I did not have, by nature,
The means to release my child.
Even at her birthing
An artificial liquid
Had to be dripped into my veins
Forcing my body to let her go.

Fourteen years later,
I find I have not changed.
I hold the umbilical cord so tight,
My daughter kicks and squirms,
Needing to be set free
From these confining quarters.
Isn't there a potion now
That will force my hand to let her go?

I Reach Up

I reach up to kiss you now.
Your wrist is thicker than mine.
Somehow,
You've surpassed me.

I don't know
If it was the tiny pillows
Of your palm,
The arch of your smooth belly,
Or your startled eyes
That reached back inside of me
To take my heart with you
On the day that you were born.
But when I held you,
I prayed, Oh, God, please
Don't ever take her from me.

What I did not know then
Is that parenting is a process
Of slowly letting go,
That the grief and joy would all
Swirl together over the years
Until the evening came
When I realized
I had to reach up
To kiss you goodnight.

Other Life

It's on an afternoon like this
That I recall
That long car drive discussion
Twenty-four years ago.

Recently married,
Propelling naively ahead,
We casually entertained the idea
Of children.

What if, in that moment,
And despite my biological urgings,
We had decided—no.
No,
Children just don't make sense for us.

Who would I be now,
All these years later?

It's hard to recall her
Or to imagine the path
She might have taken.

Maybe I'd be someone
Who made choices
Based on my own desires,
Whose heart
Actually remained inside my body.

Maybe I'd be someone
Who developed a propensity
For cleanliness and order
And predictability
In every little thing.

Maybe I'd have some money.

But we said yes,
Why not?
Lets give it a try.

So this afternoon, I am someone
Whose daughter called at seven
Last night from college
To say that she had several cavities,
One of which was throbbing
Something fierce.

Oh, God,
My child is in pain
And I am not there.

Find a strange dentist in a strange town,
Drive yourself there,
I told her,
And put it on the credit card.

Then at ten,
Just as we were going to bed,
The other daughter called.
Stranded on the highway,
Broken down car.

Her father threw on his pants
And ran out the door,
While I waited,
Imagining the worst.

She's alright, thank God.
But the car…
Put it on the credit card,
My common refrain lately.

So here I am,
Far, far away from a different,
Unimaginable life,
Right in the middle of this gloriously
Impossible mess,
Sitting on this unmade bed
Where I sneak away to write
Because my mind
Is bursting.

Nourish

Today I will serve
A feast to my family.
I will cook beautiful food
With intention
And serve it,
Like artwork,
Like abundance,
Like love,
On a platter.

And our various worlds
Will come together
For this meal.
They will eat,
And I will take them in,
Savoring
The we
And the each,
However they are now,
However we are,
Just glad for this moment.

Photographs

Paging through an album
And there I am,
A drained expression,
Glasses glaring in the flash,
Children spinning around me,
A room full of the clutter
Of toys, blankets, diapers.
I feel desperate to lend a hand
To that self I was.

There I am again
The smiling, gentle one,
My face pressed up
Against the cheek of a child,
A scene so soft
I can almost smell it.

There are a hundred more
Expressions of motherhood
That cannot be caught
By a still camera
Or a single word.

I am struck now
By the thought that ate at me
Throughout the days
I spent
Absorbed in it.
Maybe there is something else
More important
That I should be doing.

I stroke a picture of myself
Kneeling on the kitchen floor,
A crying child in each arm.
"You did well,"
I say aloud.
"You're doing alright."

Your Hands

I look at your fingers
Lingering on the chair.
I hardly recognize
Their long, delicate beds
Thin curves of a woman
That time has separated
From me.
Those fingers that once,
Thin and small,
Clung to me
For life, nourishment,
Your tight grip securing
That you would not be lost
In a bewildering world.

Now you reach for that world,
With hands formed in me
Beautifully grown
Stretching toward a life
Of your own.

I Hurt My Back

On the slippery rain soaked steps,
Frictionless flip-flops
Flying out from under me.

Now I lie flat on the couch,
Waves of pain flowing
And long, deep tears.

My grown daughter comes to comfort,
So desperately full of advice—
Cold pack,
Hot pad,
Anti-inflammatory.

What I soak in
From her soothing voice
Is love.

Thank you
For not knowing what to do,
But wanting to do something.

Your sweet attempts
Are the warm compresses
I hold to my heart.

Daughter- Leaving

The gift she will give me,
In the end, is the ability to let
Something precious,
That I had such a hand
In nurturing and protecting,
Go.

To hold back my own heart,
Afraid not just for her,
But for its own loss.

This heart,
Once full of its ownness,
Has, over the years, formed,
Beyond my own will,
And in every possible way
Around these children.
It has been rubbed smooth
And raw
By their presence.

There were times when
The weight of them
Seemed more than I could bear.
Now that her leaving is almost here,
I worry that her absence
May be heavier.

And yet,
She is strong and ready,
So full of her ownness,
That, beyond my sadness,
I rejoice for her.

You Again

We meet each other again
After all these years
Of children and responsibility,
Conversations consisting of needs
And schedules
And always,
The never enough.

Now, unexpectedly,
The children older,
We have been dropped,
Temporarily,
From the chute of duty.

Here—
On this river bank
Where, long ago,
We first learned each other.

We are learning each other again.
You, with graying hair
And reading glasses,
Me, with the odd shape
Of childbirth and menopause.

I think we are more beautiful now
For having survived
All those lustless nights,
All the energy given and drained,
All the never enough.

It is good to be with you again,
Watching the rippling river
Sparkle in the sun.

Dog

This dog
Searches and searches
Until she finds
The perfect spot—
Right on my lap.

She's just what I need now,
Someone who thinks
I am the coziest spot
In the world.

Since the kids have grown
That experience
Is only an achingly tender
Memory.

So I provide her
With a warm lap
On this cold winter evening.
She provides me
With the feeling
Of curled up contentment
Ready to adjust
To my every move.

Twenty Seven Years Later

I loved the dish drainer.
Thank you.
It was the perfect wedding gift.

It sat in my sink for many years,
Until the plastic coating
Wore off
And it left rust stains
On the porcelain.

I don't know why
I mention it now.
It's just something
I thought about
As I pulled forks and glasses
For the millionth time
From the soapy water,
Rinsed them
And set them in the drainer
To dry.

Sweet Pea

Good night, sweet pea. Sleep tight,
I call
Through her closed door.
Good night, she replies
With sleepy nonchalance.

I shuffle down the hall to bed,
Another page torn
From the calendar
Of our time together,
Which is growing thinner and thinner.

I picture cells dividing in her sleep
As she grows
From child to adult.
Way too old for the sweet pea talk
But she doesn't seem to mind too much.

Only a few short years
Until this youngest one leaves home.
I am familiar with the inevitable by now,
Fully aware that I can't slow time.

Her destination will be unique,
Full of her own dreams,
But in the end,
There will be her empty bed,
A room full of leftovers
And a heavy but proud heart
As I let go
Of this last little pea
In the pod.

25

Yesterday was the day
You were supposed to be born.
I think of it every year.
I remember feeling so forlorn
With the coming and going of that day,
Over-ready
To set down the uncomfortable weight
I carried around.

It was a long labor
When it finally came,
Harder than any birth
In the whole history of women.

Afterward, holding you,
My startlingly beautiful,
Beyond my dreams treasure,
I cried in utter relief,
"It's over,"
Meaning, of course,
The difficult part of it all.

I did not understand why the doctor laughed,
Not yet aware
That this birthing would never end.

Now

All the while
I am taking care
Of every little thing,
There is this secret self
Who dreams
And plans
For someday.

Lately,
She is impatient, though,
Tired of being put off.

There is my family,
I explain to her,
This job,
These parents.
All need to be
Taken care of.

She doesn't listen.
Go, she says, *write.*
I have waited long enough.
She is like a hungry wolf
Who won't be appeased.

I am sorry
And I am so afraid.

But when I turn to her,
When I relent,
I am utterly happy,
Ready to run with her
Into my undiscovered life.

Surprise

So it ends up
I'm not a mother
Of grown children
Whose only pitiful interest
Is their lives.

I thought I would be
But I hadn't realized
How much
The other things in life
Interest me,
Having taken
About a twenty-two year
Hiatus
From it all.

Don't ever tell the kids
But in some ways
I feel born again.

I love having them,
I loved raising them,
There's not a second of it
I would have missed,
Even the hard times.

But life is full
Of a million things
And I am not
Getting any younger.

And there is a
Particular lightness
That comes only after
Having carried a weight
So dear,
So vital,
That now carries itself
Amazingly well.

Hello Poppy Seed

My daughter,
Who not so long ago
Was a poppy seed to pollywog
That grew inside of me,
Is newly pregnant.

I imagine
The million moments of
Carrying,
Calming,
Feeding,
Adoring,
Worrying,
Astonishment,
Holding on
And letting go

That are stored in her now
Like chromosomes on a gene,
Too intricate,
Too detailed
To map.

Already I recognize
The way she walks—
Protective,
The way she speaks
About other things
But is never unaware
Of the precious secret
She holds inside.

You are blessed,
Little poppy seed.
You will grow
In a nourishing womb.
You will be born into arms
That yearn for you,
Held close by a bond
Formed long ago.

You will form her, too,
Drawing forth a self
She does not yet know
She possesses.
Your mother, my daughter,
Will learn the wonder
Of becoming.

www.ingramcontent.com/pod-product-compliance
Lightning Source LLC
Chambersburg PA
CBHW032210040426
42449CB00005B/533